# PATHWAYS
# THROUGH ACADEMIA

# PATHWAYS
# THROUGH ACADEMIA

≈

*Steven M. Cahn*

RESOURCE *Publications* · Eugene, Oregon

PATHWAYS THROUGH ACADEMIA

Resource Publications
An Imprint of Wipf and Stock Publishers
199 W. 8th Ave., Suite 3
Eugene, OR 97401

www.wipfandstock.com

PAPERBACK ISBN: 979-8-3852-4731-8
HARDCOVER ISBN: 979-8-3852-4732-5
EBOOK ISBN: 979-8-3852-4733-2

To my wife,
Marilyn Ross, MD

# CONTENTS

# PREFACE

EACH COLLEGE AND UNIVERSITY takes pride in its distinctiveness, but in many respects, their faculties are similar. They were educated in graduate school, display pedagogical skills ranging from inspiring to inept, engage more or less successfully in scholarly pursuits, participate in departmental politics, and struggle over appointment and tenure decisions.

All these aspects of a professor's life can be challenging, and in this collection of recent essays, I offer short takes on issues that arise in pursuing graduate education, teaching undergraduates, conducting research, and deliberating about issues affecting one's department and school. Note that three areas of widespread concern, curricular controversies, the tenure system, and affirmative action, are not discussed here because they are the focus of my previous book *Exploring Academic Ethics* (Wipf and Stock Publishers, 2024). Earlier versions of most of the chapters here originally appeared on the Blog of the American Philosophical Association, and I appreciate its permission to include this material.

My thanks to Wipf and Stock Publishers for continuing support of my work and especially to Savanah N. Landerholm for her expert design.

I am grateful to my brother, Victor L. Cahn, playwright, critic, and professor emeritus of English at Skidmore College, for a lifetime of sound advice, literary and otherwise, and to Dr. Mary Ann McHugh, instructor in the Hugh Downs School of Human Communication at Arizona State University, for polishing the entire manuscript with her customary elegance. To my wife, I owe more than I can express in words.

One additional note: This book's cover features an image of Main Building at Vassar College in Poughkeepsie, New York. This edifice, constructed in 1861 when it housed the entire school, is now a National Historic Landmark, home to administrative offices and student rooms. On entering the campus, you face the building as I did sixty years ago when I embarked on my first full-time faculty position. I knew little about academic life but soon recognized the challenges of teaching, the significance of research, the importance of colleagues, and the role of the administration. Later, my understanding of these matters grew, but I never forgot the fulfillment I found working with Vassar's committed students and devoted faculty. Their memory has sustained me throughout my career as I have continued to explore pathways through academia.

# I

# GRADUATE SCHOOL

# I

# STARTING OUT

ALTHOUGH MOST GRADUATE DEPARTMENTS offer entering students an orientation meeting, if my department's approach is typical, the occasion is too often a lost opportunity. Here is the scene I witnessed every September for many years. Most newcomers arrived unsure or even apprehensive, but all were eager to understand more fully the situation they faced. Few faculty participated in the session, however, and those who did treated the occasion lightly, engaging in banter with one another and evincing little concern for the anxieties of the beginners.

The chair started by inviting the newcomers to introduce themselves and indicate their specialty. Those who replied with uncertainty received patronizing smiles, and the response that invariably caused snickers was "I plan to teach."

Subsequently, the faculty were asked to describe their current scholarship. The rookies listened attentively, nodding as if comprehending every word while struggling to understand much of what was said.

Next, they were invited to ask about the program but, being unfamiliar with it, did not have much to contribute. The message they received, though, was clear and emphatic: Find an area of research and publish as much as possible. Although nearly all the doctoral students would eventually teach undergraduates, not a word was said about that responsibility. Nor was any advice given about how best to survive the travails of doctoral study. Indeed, the session concluded early when the chair announced with satisfaction that the essentials had been covered and the time had come for wine and cheese.

Perhaps this approach to orientation is unique to my program, but I presume others engage in similar practices. I would suggest, though, that we can do better. Here is advice that should prove useful to those beginning doctoral work:

1. Read widely. As a college student you were responsible only for works the instructor assigned, but as a scholar you create your own reading lists. The more literature you master, the less reliant you are on faculty.

2. Write frequently. Putting one's ideas into written form aids precise thinking. If you doubt the effectiveness of your style, consult an appropriate handbook.[1]

3. Don't delay. Do not allow lack of confidence to lead you to defer fulfilling requirements, taking examinations, or submitting papers. The longer you wait, the more the pressure mounts. Postponement is not progress.

4. Meet the professors. Eventually you will need to choose an advisor to guide work on your dissertation. Whether by attending a lecture, conversing at a departmental function, or visiting during office hours, seek a professor whose interests and personality are in sync with your own.

5. Meet other students. They can offer helpful advice about professors and strategies. Furthermore, discussion with colleagues is one of the pleasures of the profession. Granted, solitude may stimulate creativity, but scholars do not flourish in isolation, Rather, they rely on publishers, librarians, and one another.

---

1. See, for example, Steven M. Cahn and Victor L. Cahn, *Polishing Your Prose: How to Turn First Drafts into Finished Work* (New York: Columbia University Press, 2013).

6. Meet professional colleagues. Those at other institutions who share your interests can offer valuable contacts. You can encounter such individuals at scholarly conferences, whether you merely attend or, better yet, serve as a speaker, commentator, or session chair. Volunteers are often sought for these positions. Because almost all the attendees will be active scholars in your field, they will be as eager to meet you as you are to meet them.

7. Seek a dissertation topic. As you proceed, be alert for a potential project that is engaging, appropriate in scope, and original without being eccentric. Choosing your subject wisely is a crucial step toward finishing your work in a reasonable time and maximizing your chances for a desirable academic position. Publishing along the way is a plus, but finding a winning dissertation topic is invaluable.

8. Diversify your interests. Don't be a one-trick pony, a scholar with only one area of expertise who offers endless variations on the same theme. At an interview, you may well be asked about your interests apart from your dissertation. You should have a couple you can discuss.

9. Plan to teach. Before long, you will be expected to assume the obligations and challenges of instructing undergraduates. Not all your students will have an immediate attraction to your subject. Thus, as you proceed, consider how you might motivate students to explore central issues in your discipline.

10. Maintain your dignity. Unfortunately, graduate professors occasionally mistreat students in various ways, including destructive criticism, inordinate delays in returning work, inaccessibility, or failing to separate professional and personal concerns. Even worse, professors have been involved in scandals involving sexual harassment or abuse. Students should report serious incidents of mistreatment to the appropriate administrator. Thereafter, inaction from the authorities should be met with firm protest.

An orientation that explained these points might take a while but would be worth attending, especially if the session emphasized to all that the primary aim of doctoral education should not be enhancing faculty interests or prerogatives but, instead, supporting students in their efforts to succeed as scholars and teachers. As for the refreshments, they'll wait.

# 2

# CRITERIA FOR ACADEMIC SUCCESS

THOSE WHO PURSUE A professorial career typically follow a path from high school to college to graduate school to faculty membership. Rarely noted, though, is that along the way the criteria for academic success change.

To excel in high school calls for absorbing materials from various areas of inquiry, including mathematics, science, history, literature, and foreign language. Those who master these varied topics are likely to graduate with distinction and compete for admission to preferred colleges.

There they are again expected to absorb a variety of subjects. While college courses are usually more demanding than high school offerings, the criteria for success are similar.

After college, students seeking a career in academia proceed to graduate school, where they find a striking change. The previous emphasis on breadth is replaced by a stress on depth. If, for example, you enroll in a graduate English department, then you are not required to grasp other subjects, such as mathematics, science, or history. Indeed, you may know little about any fields other than English literature yet be a standout in graduate school based on the high quality of your work in literary analysis.

This narrowing of focus intensifies during your faculty career. Suppose you are a professor of English, specializing in Chaucer.

In that case, no one will be concerned with whether you have any knowledge of US foreign policy, Beethoven's string quartets, or the mind-body problem. Of overriding concern, rather, is the originality and importance of your work on Chaucer as judged by Chaucer scholars. Even if you are recognized for having written essays illuminating the writings of George Eliot or Thomas Wolfe, this accomplishment is subordinate to the quality of your work on Chaucer.

Note that knowledge of secondary literature is not apt to suffice for an outstanding professional reputation. The key question remains: Have you produced a series of notable insights admired by specialists? If not, then you are unlikely to be held in the highest regard by the scholarly community.

Granted, mastery of two or more academic disciplines is an impressive achievement that may lead a scholar to develop an influential rethinking of at least one of those areas. The danger, however, is that someone claiming to be knowledgeable in more than one field may not be recognized by experts as proficient in any.

Consider, for example, the following situation that arose while I was serving as an administrator. (The identity of the individual involved and the fields in question are masked.) Arthur, a candidate for a tenured position, presented himself as both an art historian and a philosopher. In view of his claim to dual mastery, I asked that he deliver two lectures, one to the art history department and another to the philosophy department. The results might have been predicted. The art historians were impressed by Arthur's knowledge of philosophy but not by his grasp of art history; the philosophers were impressed by his knowledge of art history but not by his grasp of philosophy. Consequently, he was not invited to join the faculty.

In sum, the breadth of interests rewarded in high school and college is neither necessary nor sufficient for success in graduate school or a professional career. To use an analogy from the world of track and field, high school and college are like a decathlon in which contestants need to display ability in ten different events. In graduate school and beyond, you choose your best event and are judged on it alone. Any weaknesses you may have in other areas are of little account.

Were you flummoxed by calculus? The experts in English don't care. Did you have trouble mastering French idioms? The experts in English don't care. Was macroeconomics a problem for you? Again, the experts in English don't care. Nor are they concerned with your SAT scores, your undergraduate GPA, any honors you may have received at college graduation, or a postgraduate fellowship you may have won. Their focus is the quality of work you have produced in their field. Only if it is considered first-rate are you widely recognized as having achieved scholarly success.

No wonder those who receive the highest grades in high school or college do not always attain professional preeminence. Nor do leading scholars invariably look back on outstanding performance prior to graduate school. Thus, we should expect that changes in the criteria for success will result in some early standouts finding themselves in lagging careers, while others who begin with undistinguished records may discover a fitting field of specialization and eventually receive acclaim. Awareness of such reversals of fortune should keep some from becoming overconfident and others from yielding to despair.

# 3

# SELECTING A SPECIALTY

FINDING AN APPROPRIATE AREA of specialization can make or break an academic career. Consider, for instance, two of my former doctoral advisees who as graduate students had superb academic records. The first chose to specialize in philosophy of religion, having already published extensively in that field. Unfortunately, the student received no offers of a faculty position and eventually pursued a non-academic path. The second had no publications but after weighing several areas of interest decided to maximize employment possibilities by specializing in ethics. Having done so, this student received two offers and went on to enjoy success in academic life.

Why did the two fare so differently? Consider a few statistics.[1] In a recent year, 164 positions were posted announcing searches for tenure-track assistant professorships in philosophy. How many specified ethics as a field of interest? Fifty-two. How many specified philosophy of religion? Two. Granted, more applicants specialized in ethics than in philosophy of religion; nevertheless, the odds did not favor anyone who worked in the latter field. Nor did philosophers of language or aestheticians fare much better, for they found only eight and four possibilities, respectively.

---

1. These were compiled by Charles Lassiter, a professor of philosophy at Gonzaga University. See charleslassiter.net.

Why were so many positions announced in ethics and so few in these other fields? The obvious answer is that far more courses are taught in some aspect of ethics than in philosophy of religion, philosophy of language, or aesthetics. These subjects are equally worthy, but at most schools, student demand for them is not especially strong.

While the number of openings in any particular area will vary from year to year, departments need to provide coverage for the courses they offer, and curricula rarely change dramatically. Admittedly, no one should be expected to alter intellectual interests to match the market. Yet a student concerned with both ethics and philosophy of religion, for instance, would enhance the possibility of finding an academic position by choosing a dissertation topic in ethics, even if later deciding to specialize in philosophy of religion.

Such was the career trajectory of one of my doctoral advisors, Arthur Danto. Until he earned tenure, he worked primarily in action theory, philosophy of science, and philosophy of history. Thereafter, his long-standing passion for the visual arts came to the fore and became the focus of virtually all his writing, resulting in his earning an international reputation as a leading art critic and philosopher of art.

In any case, graduate students should consider such statistics in their discipline. They are not decisive but allow a judgment to be made in light of the best available evidence.

# 4

# CHOOSING
# A DISSERTATION TOPIC

ONCE A DECISION IS made about an area of specialization, the
challenge arises to find a dissertation topic of appropriate scope
and depth. What should be kept in mind is that a suitable subject
needs to be effective not only in attaining a degree but also in obtaining an academic position. Yet a topic that helps achieve the
first objective may hinder success in reaching the second.

Consider a student, Chris, who specializes in ethics and is
attracted to the moral theory of Nicolai Hartmann, a rarely discussed German ontologist who viewed values as unchanging ideal
entities. As a dissertation topic, this subject may work because few
faculty members are likely to be familiar with the details of Hartmann's position or be especially concerned with the presentation
of its fine points. When Chris seeks positions in ethics, though,
most other applicants will have written dissertations devoted to
subjects far more likely to be considered relevant to interaction
with undergraduates.

A second student, Robin, wishes to be distinctive by choosing
a topic that is outré. One proposed to me years ago was a defense
of reducing crime by reinstating severe corporal punishment. Perhaps a couple of faculty members in Robin's department, finding
such a topic bold though odd, might pass the thesis. At interviews,
however, when asked to explain the work, Robin is apt to face a

skeptical audience, uncomfortable in appointing a faculty member who holds such a strange view.

A third student, Leslie, has two major research interests: the history of modern philosophy, Descartes to Kant, and the history of Russian philosophy. The former subject is taught in virtually every department, whereas the latter is offered in hardly any. Many positions, therefore, call for a specialization in modern philosophy, while virtually none mentions Russian philosophy. Hence, even if Leslie's doctoral faculty includes a specialist in Russian philosophy who encourages students to make that area the focus of their dissertations, Leslie would be well-advised to resist such urgings and choose a topic in the history of modern philosophy.

In sum, a dissertation topic that may be effective in earning a degree may prove a stumbling block in the search for a faculty position. After all, that challenge is arduous enough without presenting a dissertation topic that does not appear to fit the central needs of most departments.

# 5

# A GRADUATE STUDENT'S NIGHTMARE

THOSE WHO SUPERVISE OR assess dissertations should recognize that the power they exercise is easily abused and can result in the destruction of careers. As illustration, I offer a story grounded in facts but with details altered to protect identities.

A PhD candidate, Ari, was seeking a doctorate in English and proposed writing a dissertation analyzing the works of the playwright Harold Pinter. As it happened, the department's specialist in twentieth-century British literature did not believe Pinter an important enough figure to merit a dissertation. Ari argued at length, but the professor would not yield despite admitting never having read or seen a play by Pinter. Facing this roadblock, Ari approached another professor in the department who was not a specialist in the field but was willing to supervise the dissertation. After more than a year, the work was completed, then approved by the advisor. At that point, the professor who had balked at the topic was appointed to Ari's doctoral committee and insisted that the dissertation be expanded to include a chapter comparing and contrasting the plays of Pinter with those of Chekhov.

Months later, after the chapter was finished, the professor who demanded it declared Ari's new version unsatisfactory and insisted that it be expanded, even though the dissertation would then run more than 500 pages. Once the additional work was done, a defense was scheduled, but a dispute developed between Ari's advisor and the professor who didn't like the topic. The other members of the committee did not wish to antagonize either of the two senior professors, and finally an agreement was reached that the dissertation would need to be approved by both professors, including the one opposed to it. Ari appealed that decision to the department chair and to the dean of students, but neither would intervene. At that point Ari, enraged and exhausted, judged the situation hopeless and decided to abandon the dissertation and change career paths.

Thus, the nightmare ended. Ari left the school, and the faculty and administrators involved moved on to other matters.

Yet the story does not end there. Several years later, a member of the faculty in another department who was aware of the case and continued to be dismayed by the injustice of the outcome heard that a new chair had been appointed in the Department of English. That faculty member who had never forgotten Ari approached the chair and told the tale. The chair then shared the news that the professor opposed to the topic had recently retired, and the chair agreed that if Ari were willing to resume work, the matter could be reopened. The concerned faculty member managed to contact Ari, who despite misgivings was persuaded to try again. Another member of the department who was asked to serve as advisor expressed willingness to do so if Ari agreed to reduce the length of the dissertation by half, a step Ari was pleased to take. Then a new committee was formed, all its members approved the dissertation, a defense was scheduled, and Ari easily passed. Eventually, the dissertation was published by a well-known press.

The ending was happy, but the process unconscionable. These events suggest that all departments should have in place a committee of senior faculty members to adjudicate cases of students who at any stage in their graduate careers believe themselves aggrieved. The faculty who serve on that committee should be willing, if warranted, to rule against any departmental colleagues, no matter how distinguished.

Furthermore, an additional safeguard should be established: a college-wide faculty committee dedicated to considering student appeals of departmental decisions. To those who might reject this idea on the grounds that the agenda of such a committee would be flooded, I would reply that such a phenomenon would itself be the clearest evidence of the need for the committee.

Just as departments are required to obtain the school's approval for curricular changes, faculty appointments, or tenure and promotion decisions, so the same should be true for responses to student appeals. While checks and balances are a familiar guard against misuse of government power, they would likewise help restrain abuse of academic authority.

Admittedly, adding two levels of review does not guarantee an appropriate outcome, but at least the first level brings in the judgments of those not personally involved in the matter, and the second relies on the assessments of individuals not subject to departmental politics. Although no system is foolproof, schools can at least take steps to enhance the chances tor students to be treated fairly.

# II

## TEACHING

# 6

# A QUESTION FOR TEACHERS

IN MEETING THE CHALLENGE of offering successful instruction, here is a key question: When you prepare to teach a class, is your primary focus on the subject, assuming that students will appreciate its details, or is your primary focus on the students, seeking ways to show why the subject should matter to them?

Teachers who concentrate on the subject may find that its presentation leaves the class uninterested and unresponsive. Consequently, those instructors may suppose that their students lack intellectual capacity or scholarly commitment.

A teacher who concentrates on the students seeks to link the subject to their lives. If that connection can be established, the class is likely to become engaged.

Such an approach does not imply neglecting or distorting the subject but only finding ways to relate it to student concerns. After all, not every lecture that is academically sound is pedagogically successful. Thus, knowing a subject does not imply knowing how to teach it effectively. The latter skill requires finding ways to stimulate and maintain interest, a key reason why teaching is hard.

The task is rendered more difficult for beginning teachers who come directly from graduate school, where the emphasis is almost exclusively on mastering details of scholarly subjects. There, concentration on relatively esoteric matters is not only accepted but expected. For example, I devoted a section of my dissertation to assessing Jaakko Hintikka's reconstruction of the Master Argument for fatalism offered by Diodorus Cronus, a young contemporary of Aristotle. Yet spending the time needed to explain such material to an introductory class would be unwise.

Perhaps that possibility appears far-fetched, but I am reminded of the candidate who, at an interview I attended, was asked which readings he would assign to students taking their first course in philosophy. His confident reply: "I would start with Wittgenstein's *Blue and Brown Books*." That impractical choice of a work discussed primarily by specialists suggested a lack of understanding or concern about the capabilities and interests of students.

As an example of providing motivation, consider the classic issue of whether the principle that every event has a cause is compatible with our sense of ourselves as free agents. Complications abound, but rather than beginning with them, a promising idea is opening with a discussion of the famous 1924 Leopold and Loeb case in which their lawyer, Clarence Darrow, argued successfully that the boys, due to their upbringing, were not to blame for the murder they committed. The obvious follow-up is to consider whether any of us is ever morally responsible. Most students find that matter pertinent to understanding their own lives and the actions of others; hence, the class is apt to become engaged.

Here is another example I found pedagogically effective. When I taught introductory students Mill's defense of free thought and discussion in chapter two of *On Liberty*, I didn't begin by talking about Mill or his book. Rather, I asked the class to suppose that upon entering the building, they saw a table where passersby were invited to sign a letter, addressed to the administration, demanding that an invited speaker with a well-documented record of having expressed racist and sexist views not be allowed to appear. When I inquired which students would sign, most were sure they would, and the few holdouts quickly lost confidence in their position as others accused them of insensitivity to the feelings of those who had been victims of injustice.

At that point, I posed the question, "Would John Stuart Mill sign the letter?" Suddenly, the students recognized the significance of Mill's defense of free expression, and they agreed that Mill would refuse to sign. Then I asked students to explain Mill's view, and the discussion proceeded apace. This approach did no disservice to the complexities surrounding free speech but made apparent the connection between Mill's text and the students' own sphere of experience, thus stimulating concern for the topic.

Granted, establishing such a link is easier with some subjects than others, but successful instructors find ways. They ask themselves, "Why should students care about the material I am teaching?" The answer is likely to suggest an effective way to present it.

In sum, you don't merely teach a subject; rather, you teach a subject to students, and the test of your effectiveness is whether they learn it and view it positively. If they fail to do so, then your knowledge, however profound, has not sufficed for success in the classroom.

# 7

# THE VALUE OF VARIETY

A KEY MOMENT IN planning a course is deciding what material to cover. In this regard, I recently came across the following argument: "To me, Socrates and Plato are the greatest philosophers in the history of Western philosophy. If I am right, there could be no better introduction to philosophy than studying their theories."[1] The author then recommends an introductory course in which students are asked to read eleven dialogues of Plato: *Symposium, Phaedrus, Lysis, Euthyphro, Apology, Theaetetus, Republic, Charmides, Protagoras, Phaedo,* and *Crito.*

Let's assume the truth of the premise. Does the conclusion follow? Compare this analogous argument:

> To me, J. S. Bach is the greatest composer in the history of music. If I am right, there could be no better introduction to music than studying his compositions. Hence, I recommend that a first course focus on the following works by Bach: a cantata, an orchestral suite, a Brandenburg Concerto, a toccata and fugue for organ, a suite for solo cello, a partita for solo violin, the Concerto for Two Violins, and selections from the Goldberg Variations, the St. Matthew Passion, the Mass in B Minor, and the Art of Fugue.

1. Sahar Joakim, "Introduction to Philosophy," *APA Blog* (May 29, 2019).

The problem in both cases is that the eminence of a particular figure does not imply the pedagogical appropriateness of offering beginners only one main avenue to understanding the subject.

The case for such a concentrated approach reminds me of a session many years ago at the Eastern Division meeting of the American Philosophical Association where Fred Feldman explained his practice of requiring students in an introductory course to read and critique only one book: Descartes' *Meditations on First Philosophy*. No doubt Professor Feldman thought highly of the work, but the problem with making it the sole reading was unintentionally revealed by his commentator, Alasdair MacIntyre. He first praised Feldman's strategy of focusing on a single masterpiece but expressed dismay that Feldman had picked the wrong one. He had selected the *Meditations* rather than MacIntyre's choice: Plato's *Republic*.

The problem is that, had MacIntyre been a student in Feldman's course, MacIntyre would have been unhappy spending the entire semester discussing a single book that he didn't find especially illuminating, while Feldman would have had the same reaction had he been a student in MacIntyre's course. In any case, even a good thing overdone can become boring, and beginners may find excruciating an entire course devoted exclusively to one book or author.

Not all students find the same material appealing; therefore, the likelihood of their responding positively is increased by providing them an array of perspectives on the subject. An advanced seminar might appropriately focus on a single text or author, but an introductory course is intended to arouse the interest of as many participants as possible, and a narrow set of readings is unlikely to achieve that goal.

Granted, courses can cover only limited ground, but varied content is a pedagogical virtue. A particular philosophy professor may be more interested in free will rather than personal identity or the existence of God, but assuming the goal is to engage students in philosophical inquiry, why not cover all three topics and perhaps spark interest in at least one? Few are inspired by every philosophical author or subject, and unfortunate, indeed, is a student who might potentially have been excited by philosophy but is not offered the opportunity to study more than the part of the field with which the instructor happens to be most comfortable.

Beginning students need to be motivated, and no one topic or author will work best for all. By offering more possibilities, chances are greater that at least some aspect of the reading will prove stimulating. Therefore, in planning an introductory course, if you are uncertain whether to provide coverage of more topics or study fewer subjects in greater depth, remember that for most beginners, variety enhances vitality.

# 8

# TWO PRINCIPLES
# OF ACADEMIC ETHICS

SOME TIME AGO, WHILE I was advising an outstanding doctoral student in her search for an academic position, she showed me her graduate school transcript. I noted that she had been awarded an A in every course but one; in that single instance, she had received a B. When I asked about that anomaly, she replied, "I knew what view the professor wanted me to defend in my paper. But I disagreed with his position and wouldn't adopt it even though I realized that as a result he would lower my grade."

Assuming this student's account was accurate, and I have every reason to believe it was, the professor in question, a leading researcher, violated two fundamental principles of academic ethics. The first is that the aim of teaching is education, not indoctrination. For a teacher to defend personal beliefs is appropriate, but regarding any disputed issue, students should be provided with the strongest reasons behind opposing positions, then encouraged to develop their own views. Forcing anyone to accept the teacher's opinion regarding a debated matter is professorial malpractice.

For instance, the teacher may be a materialist, but students should be made aware of the arguments for dualism; the teacher may be a liberal, but the students should be made aware of the arguments for a conservative position; the teacher may support abortion rights, but students should be made aware of the arguments for a right to life. Those who have not learned how to explain the reasoning used by their opponents on controversial matters have not been well-taught.

The second fundamental principle of academic ethics violated by the professor is to award grades fairly. A grade represents an expert's judgment of the quality of a student's work in a specific course and is not supposed to be affected by considerations of gender, race, nationality, physical appearance, dress, personality, attitudes, innate capacities, or previous academic record. Nor is a grade supposed to reflect whether the student agrees with the professor on any controversial matter or even on the grade itself.

If an A in political philosophy is awarded because the student tries hard, comes from an impoverished community, displays an ingratiating personality, or passionately defends the professor's opinions, then the A is hopelessly ambiguous and serves no useful purpose. If, on the other hand, the grade indicates that the student has a firm grasp of a range of issues in political philosophy, then the meaning is clear.

These two principles were exemplified for me on one occasion when I taught a graduate seminar in philosophy of religion. The class included a gentleman from India who frequently contributed insights about Hinduism. I assumed he was a Hindu and welcomed his perceptive comments regarding that religious tradition. After all the classes ended, he came to my office and expressed his appreciation for the course. When I thanked him for enriching our discussion by providing the perspective of a Hindu, he disclosed that he was not a Hindu; rather, he was a Catholic priest from a Christian community in the south of India. He explained that he had not revealed his religious identity because he did not want to inhibit anyone from expressing skepticism about Christianity.

I was surprised by the news, but he told me that while he knew I was not Christian, he believed I had done justice to those who were and had demonstrated that my assessment of anyone's work did not depend on whatever religious beliefs they might defend or oppose. I was gratified by this assurance.

# Two Principles Of Academic Ethics

Professors in every course should present the material in a balanced way and not penalize any students because they do not share the teacher's viewpoint. As a test, an instructor is well-advised to imagine that intellectual opponents were in the classroom. Would they recognize the instructor's version of their position? Would they agree that at least some of their arguments had been adequately explained? Would they recognize that the evaluations of student work were justifiable? If not, the instructor should consider making greater effort to achieve fairness.

# 9

# WHEN STUDENTS FAIL

SUPPOSE YOU ARE TEACHING a course in reasoning, and early in the semester you present the concept of a valid argument, one in which *if* the premises are true, then so is the conclusion. Hence, a valid argument can have true premises and a true conclusion, false premises and a false conclusion, false premises and a true conclusion, but not true premises and a false conclusion. Several weeks later, you give a test that includes the following question: "If what you say is false, then anything implied by what you say is also false. Explain whether this claim is correct." When grading the examinations, you are dismayed to discover that almost all the students gave the wrong answer, overlooking the validity of an argument such as "All playwrights have been English; therefore, Shakespeare was English." Does the students' widespread error incline you to consider them obtuse?

Let me suggest a more appropriate response. It is embodied in a remark by Geno Auriemma, the most successful coach in the history of women's basketball, who over four decades has transformed the University of Connecticut's team from less than mediocre into the most dominant school in the history of the sport, winning an unprecedented twelve national championships.

Reflecting recently on his approach to coaching, Auriemma remarked: "After all these years, believe it or not, I take every pass, every dribble, every cut, every single thing personally to heart, like

I didn't do a good enough job coaching, that I should have done a better job of teaching that box out. I should have done a better job of how to make that pass." When a class misunderstands an essential principle, teachers should think like Auriemma: "I didn't do a good enough job. How could I have better explained that matter?"

Such would be the reaction of an elementary school teacher who found that a class of second graders were having trouble understanding multiplication. In that case, the instructor would not try to blame the students for insufficient mathematical talent but would admit that in some way the teaching had been inadequate. The same conclusion should be reached when a professor reports that most beginning students were unable to grasp why an argument with false premises and a true conclusion might nevertheless be valid.

What could be the source of the problem? Perhaps the instructor did not find a way to arouse or maintain the students' interest, did not present the material in a sequence that promoted understanding, or did not make the ideas clear due to speaking too quickly, using unfamiliar terms, or omitting steps in reasoning. Or maybe the presentation did not offer memorable examples, did not encourage questions from the class, or did not address the needs of other than the best students.

Granted, even the finest teachers do not always succeed; sometimes a presentation falls flat. But in that circumstance, the conscientious instructor does not blame the students but takes responsibility and tries to make needed pedagogical adjustments that will work better in future sessions.

Here again we have something to learn from Auriemma. In other than their unprecedented six undefeated seasons, his teams sustained at least one loss, but over thirty years, they didn't lose two consecutive games. Instead, a loss led the coach to consider what he did wrong and make needed changes to improve his team's play. Likewise, when students perform poorly on tests, teachers should be led to consider what they did wrong and make appropriate adjustments to enhance the students' level of learning.

Admittedly, individual students sometimes bear primary responsibility for not succeeding. When, however, many in the class do poorly, the most likely explanation is the ineffectiveness of the instruction; hence, a teacher seeking to understand what caused the problem should begin with a candid self-examination.

Here's one other lesson that Auriemma offers. While some commentators explain his unmatched winning percentage by arguing that he merely recruits the best players, a rival coach offered this insightful assessment: He doesn't always recruit the best players, but he consistently turns the players he recruits into the best they can be.

Analogously, the finest teacher doesn't always work with the best students but tries to guide all into fulfilling their individual potential. Thus, when a class fails to make progress, their teacher has also failed. And when students consistently succeed, their teacher also deserves credit.

# IO

# ASKING EFFECTIVE QUESTIONS

In an oral examination, faculty members are probing the breadth and depth of a student's knowledge. The usefulness of the format, however, depends on the quality of the questions. An ineffective one begins with an elaborate preamble, then goes on at length to raise multiple issues.

Suppose, for example, a student, working on the problem of free will and determinism, defends the view that the two concepts are compatible. A loquacious faculty member might begin the questioning as follows:

> The other day I was rereading the views on free will developed by W. T. Stace. Have you heard of him? He was an Englishman who taught at Princeton and was the author of many books, including *The Concept of Morals*, which I especially like. In any case, he argued that free actions are those caused by psychological states of the agent while unfree acts are caused by states of affairs external to the agent. Stace concluded that, once this distinction is understood, obviously people sometimes act of their own free will. He recognized that there are puzzling cases, but I won't take the time now to develop them. So let me ask you: Do you accept the distinction as Stace drew it? Do you think his approach offers the most effective way to draw the distinction? Do you recognize

      any cases in which the distinction is problematic? Also, is
      Stace's view in accord with Hume's approach to the issue?

This question is a failure. It takes too long to get started, goes on at too great length, and involves too many parts.

Yet how can you determine the extent of a student's knowledge of such a complex subject with a simple question that takes only a few seconds to ask? Here's a query guaranteed to do the job: "You are defending the compatibility of freedom and determinism. What do you consider the best arguments against your position?"

The first response is likely to be: "I don't know any," to which an obvious reply is: "Some philosophers of the first rank have argued against compatibilism. What reasons have they offered?"

Once the student develops the opposing position, a follow-up asks for an explanation of the counterarguments. The student is apt to continue with zest until the next question: "How would your opponents reply to your counterarguments?" A student who is then at a loss lacks firm control of the issues. After all, as John Stuart Mill wrote, "He who knows only his own side of the case knows little of that."[2]

Many years ago, a colleague of mine who delighted in asking convoluted questions approached me after an oral exam where he had talked incessantly. He asked what I thought of the student's answers. I replied that I couldn't say because the one asking the questions talked more than the one who was supposed to be answering them. My colleague laughed self-consciously and replied that I had a point.

In sum, when asking a question at an oral exam, omit any preamble, keep your remarks short, and avoid multiple queries. The others present will be grateful.

One additional note. These guidelines also apply to asking questions at a colloquium. There, members of the audience who choose to participate should avoid giving a speech or raising a host of issues. Instead, the challenge is to ask a single, concise query that focuses on a crucial aspect of the presentation. Not many faculty members can do so. They deserve our admiration.

    2. *On Liberty,* 2:23.

# III

## RESEARCH

# II

# WHY SCHOLARSHIP MATTERS

IF SCHOLARSHIP *MEANS* CONTINUED study of one's subjects, then its importance is clear. After all, an individual entrusted with guiding others has the responsibility to stay well-informed, and in an intellectual discipline, that commitment involves keeping abreast of developments as reported or discussed in scholarly books and journals.

When we seek legal counsel, we have a right to expect that our attorney is knowledgeable about recent court decisions and does not rely solely on cases studied in law school. Analogously, students are entitled to assume that their instructor does not merely repeat stale ideas but is able to provide an informed account of the most promising lines of recent thought. A PhD signifies that, as of the date awarded, the recipient has mastered a discipline. That degree, however, does not grant the holder a lifetime exemption from scholarship. A professor who depends on tattered, yellowed notes reflecting timeworn thinking is as guilty of malpractice as the physician who relies on antiquated treatments. Both are ideal candidates for early retirement.

While faculty members are obliged to keep up with their fields, need they also make original contributions? For those whose teaching is confined to the introductory level and who would typically hold appointments at two-year colleges, a requirement to publish is not justified on pedagogic grounds. Someone can be a superb teacher of calculus without having authored papers in the frontiers of mathematics. A similar point can be made about those who specialize in teaching introductory foreign language, English composition. or other such courses. Indeed, a doctoral degree need not be a prerequisite for handling these assignments. Teaching prowess along with up-to-date knowledge of the subjects and the methodologies for their presentation should suffice.

In contrast, most members of a four-year college or university faculty are expected to be able to work with all students, including those enrolled in specialized courses, advanced seminars, or independent study. In the case of these professors, the writing of books or articles relates directly to their pedagogic responsibilities.

Such activity helps hone skills in formulating creative ideas with care and precision. Not every notion that sounds convincing in conversation can survive the scrutiny endured by the written word, especially when the readers are experts. Those instructors expected to provide original perspectives in the classroom ought to have their ability to do so evaluated periodically in accord with rigorous standards maintained by peers who referee manuscripts for publication and comment on materials when they appear. For scholars to submit their work for such review is the equivalent of pilots undergoing periodic testing. In both cases, professionals are examined to determine whether their skills remain at the level necessary for the proper fulfillment of their duties.

All faculty members capable of conducting research are obligated to do so for another reason. Professors profess the worth of their subjects, and no subject can thrive in the absence of original contributions. No one is better qualified than professors to provide such sustaining creativity. Publications, then, ought to result from a faculty member's commitment to the progress of a discipline.

Granted, few contributors will produce revolutionary breakthroughs, and most can make only modest advances. If the intellectual life is to thrive, though, numerous scholars need to contribute to its growth. Even those blessed with genius build on the work of predecessors, weigh the comments of colleagues, and bequeath to successors the task of tracing the consequences of momentous insights. Faculty members able to contribute should therefore heed the injunction of an ancient Hebrew sage: "It is not your duty to complete the task, but you are not free to desist from it."[1]

This expectation that professors contribute to the scholarly literature has often been summed up in the familiar phrase "publish or perish." Some find this policy objectionable, but few who oppose it would object to the expectation that faculty members "think or perish," yet to publish is to make available to all the results of one's best thinking. Professors who fail to do so should seek alternative ways of providing clear and substantial evidence of their intellectual vigor. If they are unable to shoulder the burden of proof, others are justified in doubting the quality of their thinking and their teaching.

---

1. *Ethics of the Fathers*, trans. Hyman Goldin (New York: Hebrew Publishing Company, 1962), 2:21.

# 12

# WHY RESEARCH RULES

PUBLISHING THE RESULTS OF research is the most prestigious aspect of a professor's responsibilities. Those who excel at it are invited to accept appointments at leading institutions, deliver named lectures, and receive other honors.

For that reason, faculty consider scholarship to be the core of the academic enterprise. Even those who have few academic accomplishments regard themselves as experts whose pursuit of knowledge is the essence of their work. Although they may never complete any research, when asked about scholarly projects, they always claim to be working on one. Only a neophyte would admit, "I don't have any." Indeed, scholarship is recognized as so important that if a faculty member is asked to take on a departmental responsibility, the one negative reply that is invariably accepted runs along these lines: "I'd be happy to, but I have an article I need to finish." That explanation points to a duty that supersedes all others.

When asked what they do for a living, professors don't identify themselves as teachers but as physicists, economists, literary critics, and so on. Their primary commitment is to their discipline, not their classes.

Indeed, few faculty members would not welcome a reduction in their instructional hours, known in the jargon as a "load." Research, incidentally, is never referred to as a "load" but as an "opportunity." Thus, a professor might say to colleagues, "Good news.

My teaching load has been reduced, so I'll finally have time for my own work."

Of course, faculty depend for their salaries on tuition dollars, but this reliance on the presence of students is of minor concern to professors. After all, teaching and advising students take away from time better spent devoted to the faculty's own specializations.

Whereas students seek inspiring teachers, most professors seek professional recognition. These goals do not necessarily align, explaining why the quality of instruction in college and universities is often disappointing.

Granted, more professors than might be supposed care about the quality of the instruction they offer. Yet while their students recognize that concern and find ways to express their appreciation,[1] the efforts to teach well are unlikely to win plaudits from colleagues or administrators. They mouth platitudes about the importance of teaching but nevertheless have no doubt that in the world of academia, research rules.

---

1. See, for example, *Bronx Socrates: Portrait of a Legendary Teacher,* ed. Steven M. Cahn (Eugene, OR: Wipf and Stock Publishers, 2024).

# 13

# WHY RESEARCH SHOULDN'T RULE

IN A GENEROUS REVIEW of my recent book *Professors as Teachers*,[1] Martin Benjamin supports most of its major contentions, yet he finds outdated my claim that research, not teaching, rules in academia.[2] In response, he details how the field of philosophy has taken steps to emphasize teaching. These include the founding of specialized organizations and journals as well as the sponsorship of numerous conferences and workshops.

Such activities are admirable, but they are consistent with my view that in academia, scholarship is central whereas unfortunately teaching is peripheral. For instance, a top-notch researcher who is barely adequate in the classroom is far more likely to be appointed, promoted, or awarded tenure, compared to a superb teacher whose scholarly record is thin.

This phenomenon is not surprising, given that all members of a department share in the prestige of having on its roster a national or international authority, whereas the presence of a celebrated teacher can be perturbing to colleagues. After all, how many faculty are comfortable admitting that someone else's class size is larger due to that individual's superior pedagogic skills? In such a situation, the inclination is to chalk up success to mere personal popularity or generous grading.

1. Wipf and Stock Publishers, 2022.
2. *Teaching Philosophy*, 46:3, 2023, 405–409.

Administrators, too, favor the renowned researcher over the best of instructors. The celebrated scholar focuses wide attention on the institution and in some disciplines may attract outside funding that contributes significantly to the school's coffers. For that reason, leading researchers regardless of their teaching performance have far more leverage with the administration than those faculty who excel primarily in the classroom.

How would we know if teaching were taken more seriously? One sign would be if graduate schools required that all students seeking teaching positions demonstrate teaching prowess as evaluated by peer review, either in a departmental practicum or in an extended series of classroom observations. In that case, letters of recommendation from the department would include detailed accounts of a candidate's teaching, not just a perfunctory remark such as, "I have never seen this individual teach, but I presume the classroom performance will be fine." Unfortunately, such an optimistic prediction is without basis.

A second sign would be if schools making appointments were more concerned with evidence of teaching skill. Thus, during campus interviews, each candidate would be expected not only to give a research paper but also to deliver a talk on an elementary topic, organized and presented as if the audience were introductory students. Only those candidates whose teaching was proficient would be given serious consideration.

Third, on those occasions when colleagues routinely undertake an elaborate review of a professor's research, so too would they engage in a thorough evaluation of a professor's work in the classroom. Departmental colleagues would visit classes and examine written materials. After all, the more an institution is concerned with teaching, the more effort would be made to assess it.

Fourth, as faculty are given release time to pursue their research, so they would be given release time to develop new courses, syllabi, and methods. They would also be offered the opportunity to attend a center for teaching effectiveness, working to strengthen their pedagogic skills with the guidance of master teachers.

Fifth and finally, suppose that in considering faculty for salary raises or other recognitions, concern for quality of teaching were counted more heavily. Granted, some institutions give teaching prizes to a select few while rewarding research for the many, but I doubt that any school gives research prizes to a select few while rewarding teaching for the many.

In sum, imagine that from day one, graduate students were reminded of their obligations as teachers, were expected to work at enhancing their teaching skills, and were persuaded that the quality of their teaching throughout their careers would play a major role in their academic success. Then teaching would not be overshadowed by research but would be illuminated for all to appreciate.

# IV

## DEPARTMENTS

# 14

# HOW DEPARTMENTS FUNCTION

A PROFESSOR'S APPOINTMENT IS not simply to a school's faculty but also to a particular department, and to paraphrase the opening of *Anna Karenina,* all happy departments are alike, but each unhappy department is unhappy in its own fashion.

The ideal is a friendly department where colleagues who might disagree intellectually nevertheless provide mutual support, share pedagogical advice, comment on one another's scholarly papers, and work together for the common good. In such an atmosphere, students are able to pursue their studies without the detrimental effects of personal animosities among the faculty.

Yet other departments are damaged by discord. In one, authoritarian rule leads to resentment and eventual rebellion, while in another, infirm leadership results in anarchy. Some are beset by hostile factions engaged in a variety of personal, political, or scholarly disputes. Although the origins of such battles may be shrouded in ancient history, the feuds live on and continue to divide members. In such struggles, students are typically used as pawns, and their academic needs are virtually forgotten.

The departmental cast of characters include those who stress research, those who focus on teaching, those who perform much school service, and some who excel in two or even all three areas. Unfortunately, a few faculty members are barely adequate in any.

I myself have had as colleagues such memorable figures as a crusty old-timer with few publications who taught the same courses with the same reading lists for decades; a fading scholar whose alcoholism began to overshadow his considerable academic achievements; a successful writer and teacher who became disengaged from departmental responsibilities and left to join the faculty at a lesser-known school to obtain a better pension plan; a prolific scholar who was eventually consumed by debauchery; a sincere but ineffective teacher without scholarly ambition who inherited a fortune and lost interest in academic pursuits; a fine scholar and strong teacher whose work was gradually overtaken by a passion for radical politics; and a beginner who published papers in prestigious journals but found academic life unfulfilling and embarked instead on a promising career as a lawyer.

An additional complication is that faculty in the same department may approach their common discipline with strikingly different interests and methodologies. I recall an incident involving a celebrated analytic philosopher who entered an elevator in his office building and found himself alone with an equally famous, old-time historian of philosophy. They exchanged not a word until coming to their common floor, then going separate ways. As the analytic philosopher later remarked, "I couldn't think of anything to say to him."

How much does an expert in Milton have in common with another who specializes in Faulkner? These two professors may reside in the same department yet have little in common.

Students often suppose that, although they find difficulty in dealing with certain professors, faculty members themselves get along amiably. Nothing could be further from the truth. Departments can be rife with animosities, and professors may be glad they don't have to study with certain colleagues whose work they consider inadequate and whose personalities they find grating.

These tensions come to the fore in department meetings. Some might suppose that their professors, whose lives center on reasoned discussion, would behave in exemplary fashion. Such is not the case. Actually, remarkably few professors are able to transfer their scholarly skills to practical issues. Just present the group with a real-life problem, and the meeting turns into a mélange of reminiscences, irrelevancies, and impracticalities. Rarely can consensus be reached and even then probably fails to do justice to the complexities of the problem. Once in a while, however, a faculty member demonstrates the ability to think clearly and offer realistic solutions. That person is likely to become a departmental chair and, if willing, may be on track for a career in administration.

A fine philosopher once remarked that his colleagues possess "cognitive abilities of a special sort, which are...extremely sophisticated *relative* to the population norm."[1] I can only suppose he had never witnessed a department meeting.

1. Neil Levy, "Downshifting and Meaning in Life," *Ratio* 18, no. 2 (2005), 187–188.

# 15

# APPOINTMENTS

WHATEVER STRIFE MAY PERMEATE a department, when a vacancy appears, all members will urge the dean to allow it to be filled. After all, a larger department is a stronger one, for it enrolls more students and receives a greater share of administrative support. Searching for a new colleague, however, is rarely a smooth process and can intensify friction or create it where none existed.

Once informed that it can make an appointment, the department needs to develop an announcement of the position. The question then arises as to which subfields, if any, will be given prominence in the search. Ideally, the decision should reflect a fair assessment of the department's needs. Too often, though, that criterion is ignored.

Imagine a music department that has four members teaching the history of Western music. Let us designate them as A, B, C, and D. A teaches Renaissance music, B the Baroque age, C the Classical period, and D the music of the 20th and 21st centuries. What's missing?

A neutral observer would immediately recognize a crucial gap: post-Beethoven music of the Romantic period, including such leading figures as Brahms and Wagner. A candidate teaching the Romantic era, however, may not be the department's first priority.

Consider how the discussion might proceed.

A. I'm supposed to cover all of Renaissance music, but my research focuses on the early period. We need someone for the late.

B. My work is centered on Bach, but there's so much more in the Baroque. Let's add someone who specializes in other Baroque composers. The nineteenth century is important, but I haven't heard much call from students wishing to specialize in Tchaikovsky or Verdi.

C. Recently I've been concentrating on Beethoven's quartets. How about someone whose research focuses on Haydn or Mozart? We can also use someone who is willing to cover the year-long survey in the history of music.

D. Contemporary music is so varied that we need another person to do it justice. I have a friend from graduate school who has published on electronic music and would be a terrific colleague.

The pattern is clear. Every member hopes to use the appointment to advance a personal research agenda.

Here's commentary to help explain the discussion.

A. The Renaissance historian seeks a colleague with similar scholarly interests so as to have someone at hand for discussion and assistance. Rather than saying so, however, A stresses differences between the early and later Renaissance, then argues that the department needs a specialist in both. The problem, of course, is that any subject can be divided into smaller units and the argument made that each unit needs coverage. We might term this strategy "divide and augment."

B. The Baroque historian also uses the "divide and augment" strategy followed by an appeal to lack of student interest in researching nineteenth-century music. But if Baroque music weren't in the curriculum, would students complain about a lack of opportunity to focus on Corelli or Tartini?

C. The classical scholar seeks a supportive colleague who specializes in Haydn or Mozart as well as someone to teach the history of music survey that requires extensive preparation and covers materials outside any one instructor's scope. This professor proposes department members avoid that demanding assignment by handing it to a newcomer who, perhaps without much enthusiasm but in an effort to gain the position, would be willing to offer the course.

D. The contemporary music scholar uses the "divide and augment" strategy, then adds what might be labelled the "I have a friend" approach. This maneuver typically leads professors to overrate a professional pal with whom they share research interests, then become angry if colleagues do not share this view.

Once the four members of the department present their opinions, the discussion usually turns repetitive and possibly unpleasant, as each one reiterates ever more forcefully already-stated positions. In accord with academic manners, though, attacks are never launched against the value of anyone else's research area but instead framed as defenses of one's own. How is the impasse broken?

One solution calls for the advertisement to include a list of specializations sought: the later Renaissance, the Baroque age, Haydn and Mozart, the nineteenth century, and electronic music. That approach will likely satisfy the four members but appear strange to potential candidates who will wonder why the department has such an unusual set of priorities.

Here an effective dean might step in and insist that the complex advertisement be sharpened. How might the department react to the dean's objection? A common move is to declare that the search will seek the best person, regardless of field. This step will satisfy all involved but down the road produces poor results.

The reason is revelatory. Although specialists may have some acquaintance with other subject matters, only regarding their own are they familiar with a broad spectrum of faculty members, programs, and scholarly activities. Therefore, unless one candidate is clearly superior to all others (a rare situation), each professor will find "the best" to be the best in that specialist's field and try to forge a majority in favor of that candidate. As the infighting continues, the field most likely to be neglected is the one currently unrepresented; it is least known by the members yet most in need of an appointment. In the end, whichever professor is politically savvy and most determined carries the day. If after a year or two another opening appears and again the same area is disregarded, the department will become lopsided, perhaps for decades.

Why did this situation develop? Because the dean allowed the department to advertise the position as open. What should have happened? When the department suggested that compromise, a judicious and courageous dean (more about this ideal in a later chapter) should have responded, "Most of the nineteenth century is uncovered. Unless that's the specialty you announce, the search is over." The department would be upset but in order to make an appointment would likely bow to the dean.

Eventually, if the dean monitors the search process carefully, the department will settle on a candidate who focuses on the Romantic era. As a result, the students will benefit, and the faculty may eventually appreciate the perspective of their new colleague and realize the wisdom of offering broader coverage.

In any case, discord is likely to accompany the process. Indeed, if for nefarious reasons someone wanted to create turmoil in an amiable department, I cannot think of a more effective strategy than offering the members an opportunity to undertake a search. Even if they do not reach consensus, the members should at least consider themselves fortunate if their good relations survive.

# 16

# DEPARTMENTAL VOTING

HERE'S A COMMON SITUATION. A department plans to choose ten candidates to interview for one opening. From the hundreds who apply, the field is reduced to twenty-six, and at the meeting where the final vote is to occur, a professor suggests that each faculty member be given five votes, and the ten candidates receiving the most votes will be invited. All members of the department, unaware of the proposal's unfortunate consequences, agree to this apparently generous voting system.

Suppose the department has twelve members, of whom eleven prefer candidate A to all others, then B, then C, and so on to Z, who is rated the lowest. One member of the department, however, prefers the candidates in the reverse order, ranking Z the highest, then Y, then X, and so on to A, who is rated the lowest.

When the voting occurs, the result is that A through E each receive eleven votes, while Z through V each receive one vote. Thus, the top ten vote getters are A through E and Z through V, so each is invited for an interview.

Something has gone wrong. Almost all members of the department prefer A through J, and only one member prefers Z through Q, yet while A through E have been invited, F through J, who have nearly unanimous support, have been passed over in favor of Z through V, who almost no one wishes to interview.

This unwanted outcome results from violation of an essential principle of fair voting. Each voter should be given the same number of votes as the number of candidates to be selected. Therefore, in this case each member of the department should have received ten votes because ten candidates were to be chosen. Using that principle would have resulted in invitations to A through J, preferred by the overwhelming majority of the department. Z through Q were the candidates least preferred by almost all members of the department and should not have been picked.

Keep in mind, therefore, that when a department votes to choose a certain number of people for any purpose, each member should be given the same number of votes as the number of people to be selected. In that way, voting will reflect the will of the majority.

When you vote for judges on Election Day, you are entitled to cast the same number of votes as the number of judges to be elected. The same principle should apply in departmental voting.

# 17

# CONDUCTING INTERVIEWS

A CRUCIAL STEP IN making a faculty appointment is the initial interviewing of candidates. The process typically takes place at a professional meeting or by teleconference. Usually, several faculty members will talk individually for thirty to forty minutes with ten or so candidates.

Those being interviewed can perform well or poorly, but so can those conducting the interviews. Much has been written about how to be interviewed, but here I want to concentrate on how to conduct an interview.

1. Ask all applicants the same basic questions, set in advance. Follow-ups will differ in each case, but by structuring all interviews alike, a source of unfairness is minimized. Suppose, for instance, that candidate A is preferred over candidate B, and one reason is that B offered a weak answer to a particular question. If A was not asked the same question, why presume A's answer would have been better than B's? Perhaps the question itself was problematic.

2. Keep notes on what was said. As the hours wear on, attention wanders, and one candidate begins to blur into another. Weeks later, when the candidates are evaluated at a department meeting or in discussion with a dean, the written record will prove invaluable.

3. Ask one question at a time, thereby avoiding this sort of pile-up: "Why did you choose to write about Plato's Theory of Forms? What is the theory? And, by the way, what do you think of Aristotle's criticisms of the theory?"

4. Interviewers may be inclined to engage in an extended discussion of a comment made by the candidate, but that temptation should be resisted. Time is limited, and the purpose of an interview is not to offer departmental colleagues the opportunity to display their erudition. One rule of thumb: Interviewers should speak much less than the candidate.

5. Asking about a candidate's dissertation is sensible, but concentrating on it almost exclusively is limiting. How about asking: "Tell us something about your areas of interest outside the field of your dissertation." Or even: "Do you have intellectual pursuits beyond our discipline?" After all, a candidate is being considered for an appointment not only to a department but to an entire faculty. As such, the individual may be called on to participate in interdisciplinary programs, offer lectures on broad themes, or share in decisions affecting the college curriculum. Some attention, therefore, should be paid to the range of a candidate's intellectual horizon.

6. Candidates are expected to be effective teachers; hence, some pedagogical questions should be asked. For example, "All of us teach an introductory course. Which texts would you use, and what topics would you cover?" "How would you handle the responsibility of grading?"

7. Candidates are also expected to assume a fair share of the day-to-day tasks that are an inescapable part of academic life. A revealing question might be the following: "Would you be willing to serve on the curriculum committee, assessing possible changes to course offerings and reviewing requirements for the major?" If one candidate replies, "I would rather spend time on my research," and another says, "I'd be happy to help in any way I can," you've learned what you need to know.

8. Do not ask personal questions that have no bearing on performance as a faculty member. For example, "Do you think you might be too old for this position?" "Will your spouse be living with you?" If a colleague poses such an inappropriate query, other interviewers should intervene and return the discussion to suitable topics.

9. Always be polite. Never engage in insults, laugh derisively at an answer, act in a condescending manner, or display a lack of interest in the proceedings. Remember that you, too, were once an applicant.

In sum, interviewers should make every effort to be kind and fair. They should not, however, be credulous. Challenging questions should be asked, and cogent answers expected. Those candidates who do not provide them should be eliminated from consideration, not out of animosity but from a commitment to appointing new colleagues who give evidence of excelling as scholars, teachers, and contributors to the academic community.

# 18

# POLITICS AND APPOINTMENTS

LET US RETURN TO the widely accepted principle of academic ethics that candidates should not be asked questions that do not bear on performance as a faculty member. If an applicant raises inappropriate considerations, the discussion should not be allowed to continue along that path. For example, if interviewees mention their sexual orientation, the response should be that the matter is not relevant to the appointment and will not be further discussed. Furthermore, even if a candidate's vita includes such information as date of birth or number of children, these matters are not germane. Such data should not be requested, and, if provided, should not be considered.

So much is uncontroversial. Consider, however, a situation I faced some years ago when one of our doctoral students asked my advice whether to include on his vita the information that he had served as a columnist for *National Review*, a leading journal of conservative opinion.

Although I believe most professors would agree that a candidate's politics should not be considered in making an appointment, I doubted that faculty were likely to act in accord with this principle. Of course, if the doctoral student had worked for a journal of liberal opinion, he would not have been concerned about saying so. He anticipated, however, that most professors would have a negative view of someone with his political outlook.

At the time, my advice to the student was to omit the information. He did so and obtained a fine position. Perhaps the result would have been the same had he acted otherwise, but years later he wrote that my advice had been correct and that the academy suffers from what he termed "ideological rigidity."[2]

If you disagree, I urge you to test your view by considering whether your colleagues would react differently to a candidate who was a columnist for a left-leaning magazine or one who contributed regularly to a right-leaning journal,. Unless your colleagues would be unaffected in either case, politics is playing more of a role than it should in academic appointments.

2. See Daniel A. Kaufman's correspondence of July 8, 2018 to the American Philosophical Association Blog's posting of an earlier version of this essay.

# V

# THE ADMINISTRATION

# 19

# SEARCHING FOR ACADEMIC ADMINISTRATORS

EVERY YEAR NUMEROUS COLLEGES and universities conduct elaborate searches for academic administrators, including all manner of deans, vice presidents, and provosts. In each case, the steps are remarkably similar. A search committee is formed, an advertisement is placed, a hundred or so applications are received, the list is shortened, letters of reference are obtained, another cut is made, interviews are conducted that include department members or their representatives, the committee makes its recommendations, and a high-ranking official announces the outcome.

The process is invariably exhausting, but the results are often disappointing. The candidate who appeared confident, capable, and genial during interviews may turn out to be evasive, ineffective, or disagreeable. The rejected candidate whose crusty manner or candid opinions put off some committee members may be offered an administrative position elsewhere and became widely admired for trustworthiness, conscientiousness, and acumen. Some mistakes are inevitable, of course, but at least judgments should be made in the light of the best available evidence. Too often, however, committees deliberate in the dark.

They proceed as if the most important information was found in a curriculum vitae, letters from a candidate's supporters, and observations of a candidate's demeanor in a series of brief meetings.

The most reliable indicator of future performance, though, is past performance. Yet its quality is not found in a vita, a supporter's letter, or brief question-and-answer sessions.

The vita lists the positions held, not the quality of performance in each position. A committee seeking a dean may be impressed by a candidate's having been a department chair, but under that candidate's leadership did the department prosper or stagnate? Did department members work together or squabble? Was the department's curriculum regularly refreshed or outdated? The vita doesn't reveal the answers.

As for an interview, it indicates more about the candidate's surface personality and oral facility than sagacity or dependability. Speaking with assurance doesn't imply success in dealing with difficult situations. Indeed, I recall an administrator I knew who moved from one position to another, failing at each but invariably obtaining a more prestigious one due to skill in handling interviews. Only too late did a committee at each school discover its mistake.

Regarding letters of recommendation, they are notoriously unhelpful. Even Stalin could have obtained glowing letters from three of his colleagues, testifying to his consultative management style, creative planning, and sense of humor.

The best evidence is to be found not in what a candidate's friends say but in the judgments of individuals who hold responsible positions at the candidate's campus. What does the chair of the senate say about the candidate's commitment to upholding the appropriate authority of the faculty? What does the chair of the curriculum committee report about the candidate's attitude concerning degree requirements? What does the chair of the appointments committee think of the candidate's standards for appointments, promotions, and tenure? What do department chairs relate about the candidate's approach to making budgetary decisions? Do the chairs find the candidate accessible, resourceful, fairminded, and committed to enhancing academic quality? Do other administrators or administrative assistants view the candidate as thoughtful or impulsive, patient or irritable, collegial or over-bearing, forgiving or vindictive?

During an interview the candidate may maintain a false front, but those who have long observed the candidate's character, including at times of personal confrontation or institutional crisis, are beyond being fooled. They know the candidate in a way no committee can match.

Thus, when the list of finalists is determined, each should be informed that several members of the committee will speak to or better yet visit key members of the academic community at the candidate's school. While a candidate may request that a particular person not be contacted if thought to be negatively biased, a candidate who objects to the whole procedure should be passed over. For however strong the candidate's desire to retain confidentiality, it is outweighed by the committee's obligation to make the wisest possible decision.

If the information thereby obtained suggests that the administrator's performance was less than first-rate, the committee may reasonably assume the person will do no better at the next position. The administrator who micromanaged one campus is a good bet to try to do so at the next. The administrator who wasted money at one institution is unlikely to spend wisely at another. During interviews, a candidate may give the impression of welcoming constructive criticism, but if numerous colleagues report to the contrary, their testimony should be considered decisive.

Indeed, were I required to select an administrator by relying on a vita, letters of recommendation, and interviews or, rather, on the judgments of numerous previous colleagues, I would choose the latter alternative. Search committees, however, do not face this option. They can continue to consider the usual information while supplementing it with the best possible evidence. Such a procedure would lead to greater satisfaction with the performance of those we entrust with administrative responsibilities.

# 20

# DEANS

WHILE I WAS CHAIRING the philosophy department at the University of Vermont, the college undertook a search for a new dean of arts and sciences. When the finalists came to campus, department heads were invited to interview them. Realizing that candidates usually provide canned answers, I decided to ask each applicant the same two fresh questions. My first: "Should our graduates have a basic understanding of the physical structure of the world?" Each interviewee responded confidently in the affirmative. Then I continued: "Can I, therefore, assume that you favor a science requirement for the bachelor's degree?" Almost all candidates suddenly began to stammer, seeking some way to reconcile their support for the study of science with their worries about requiring it. Only one candidate, chemist John G. Jewett, responded directly: "I do favor a science requirement, plus a mathematics requirement."

Later at an informal reception, one of my colleagues approached Jewett and expressed concern about his answer.

"I'm unsure about your idea to increase requirements. Don't you think we should proceed cautiously?"

"Why?" said Jewett. "Do you have another plan?"

"No" said my colleague.

"Then why not try mine?"

I was pleased when Jewett was appointed to the position, and decades later the college still requires that undergraduates study both mathematics and science. Such is the impact of a bold and wise dean, which Jewett proved to be.

As an example of his insightful policies, I would cite his method of dealing with departments inclined to award tenure to colleagues with marginal records. Jewett addressed this typical problem by announcing a policy that proved effective. If a department turned down one of its members for tenure, then that department was automatically entitled to search for a replacement. If, however, a department approved a member for tenure but the school found the case unconvincing, then tenure was not awarded and the department was not permitted to fill the vacancy. Unsurprisingly, departments became more careful regarding their recommendations for awarding tenure.

I should add that while Jewett expressed admiration for the philosophy department, he did not always grant our requests. When I pointed to our heavy enrollment and asked for a new appointment, he replied, "If I give you one, you'll just choose another excellent teacher, and your numbers will soar even higher. Our few available lines are needed elsewhere." I couldn't disagree with his firm but reasonable response.

In sum, a school is greatly affected by the academic priorities and administrative style of its dean. Some of those who fill the position are highly effective and consequently their colleges thrive. Others deans are inadequate, and their colleges languish.

Regarding Jewett, he was described by William Mann, my superb successor in chairing the philosophy department, as "the scourge of those who despise merit." That assessment is one of which any dean should be proud.

# 21

# DIVESTITURE

ONE OF THE TOUGHEST issues facing today's administrators is a demand that the school divest from stocks some faculty and students view as morally questionable. How to deal with this situation is unclear. Who should decide the matter and on what basis? The answers are hard to discern.

Consider the fundamentals. The mission of a college or university is to develop and transmit knowledge. Doing so effectively calls for maintaining an atmosphere of free inquiry in which no one dictates that certain subjects are taboo, that certain methods of inquiry are unacceptable, or that certain conclusions are illegitimate. Whether an argument for the existence of God is sound or our government's foreign policy misguided are matters for discussion, not decree.

This open atmosphere is threatened by a school's adopting an official stance on issues unrelated to its educational mission. Doing so alienates dissenters and represses the productive disagreements that characterize intellectual inquiry.

Suppose an administration recognizes this principle but needs to decide whether to divest from the stock of a company some believe to be acting unethically. The first problem with taking such action is that selling stock is logically equivalent to someone buying it. If, though, you believe that holding a particular stock is immoral, then so is enabling a buyer to do the same. The situation is akin to possessing a dangerous toy and seeking to rid oneself of it by selling it to another family.[3]

Another fundamental problem is that cutting ties with immoral companies requires judging which are moral and which not. By doing so, the institution is in essence adopting an official stance on an issue unrelated to its educational mission, thereby again alienating dissenters and repressing disagreement.

Understandably, schools wish to grow their funds, but buying and selling individual stocks is not the only way to do so. Other investment products include treasuries, commodities, and a variety of options that do not imply anything about the moral status of any particular company.

Such approaches avoid pressuring anyone at the school to subscribe to a decision that is tantamount to either an endorsement or a rejection. Further, any call for divestment would be pointless because the school would not own the stock of any specific company..

Granted, an investment manager might over time earn a larger return for the institution by choosing individual stocks, but maximizing money is not a school's only goal. Just as a college or university should not accept a gift from anyone demanding in return control over the school's staffing or curriculum, so an increase in the probability of a greater return on investment is not worth the risk of fomenting enmity among administrators, faculty, and students.

Any specific stock may at one time be undisputed to purchase yet suddenly become controversial to own, and the demand for divestiture can quickly undermine campus comity. A wiser course for a college or university is not to own individual stocks in the first place.

3. For further discussion of this issue, see Steven M. Cahn, *A Philosopher's Journey: Essays from Six Decades*, (Eugene, OR: Wipf and Stock Publishers, 2020), 126–127.

# VI
## CONCLUSION

# 22

# FACULTY MORALE

ACCORDING TO A WELL-WORN witticism, faculty morale is always at its lowest. This quip, although at odds with my experience, suggests a question: Even if many professors are content, why are some not? I would suggest at least the following generic factors.

1. Apart from a small number of highly regarded scholars, most faculty would be unable to find a position other than the one they currently hold. In short, they lack mobility.

2. Because appointments are so difficult to obtain, most faculty are not living in the location of their choice. They reside near the school that invited them to join a department.

3. No professors participate in choosing any colleague who was tenured when they arrived. The resulting situation may be reminiscent of Sartre's *Huis Clos (No Exit)*, in which "L'enfer, c'est les autres." ("Hell is other people.")

4. Over time, teaching can become exhausting. Presenting the same material year after year, grading bushels of papers, and dealing with seemingly endless student concerns can undermine enthusiasm.

5. Research can be frustrating, progress slow, and publication chancy. Even then, the work is likely to be soon forgotten.

6. While faculty control their own classrooms and contribute to departmental curricula, administrators hold sway over the life of the institution. Faculty have little or no say regarding the distribution of money and lines or the development of external relationships.

7. Salaries are relatively low compared to those of physicians in sought-after specialties, partners in prestigious law practices, or managers in successful investment firms. Even the most illustrious professor can only dream of the level of compensation received by those who succeed along these other paths.

Yet in the face of such vexations, tenured professors enjoy unparalleled job security as well as the freedom to cultivate their own interests. No one tells them how or when to proceed with their projects; the choices are theirs. Each professor also enjoys the opportunity to work with responsive students and benefit from supportive colleagues,

Indeed, each year thousands of doctoral students strive to obtain academic positions. Presumably, those applicants believe that whatever may be the drawbacks of professorial life, they are outweighed by its advantages. Keeping these in mind should help sustain faculty morale.

# 23

# EXPRESSING APPRECIATION

ONE NOTICEABLE FEATURE OF academic life is how much time is spent arguing against the views of others. After all, for a paper to be thought worthy of presentation or an article to be considered publishable, it needs to express at least some dissatisfaction with prevailing opinion.

Such a focus on finding fault leads easily to a lack of empathy. For example, years ago I attended a departmental colloquium where the speaker offered a talk I found clear, insightful, and compelling. When the opportunity came for comments, I expressed appreciation for her fine presentation. The audience waited for my criticisms, but I had none. I merely wanted to offer a compliment. My attitude, however, appeared to shock my colleagues. Wasn't I going to try to demonstrate a mistake in her argument? Wasn't I going to suggest the limitations of her approach? Wasn't I going to call attention to a reference she had omitted? If not, why had I spoken?

Similarly, I recall that after the publication of Robert Nozick's remarkable book *Philosophical Explanations,* I saw him at a national meeting of the American Philosophical Association where I told him how much I admired his new work.[1] Then I apologized for repeating what he had surely heard many times before. To my

1. Robert Nozick, *Philosophical Explanations* (Cambridge, MA: Harvard University Press, 1981).

surprise, he replied ruefully that, in fact, I was the first person there to have complimented him. Others had sought him out but only to express disagreements; no word of encouragement had passed their lips.

Not offering appreciation when merited indicates a lack of manners, a failure to treat others appropriately. The link between manners and ethics was noted by Thomas Hobbes, who referred to manners as small morals,[2] an insight John Dewey expressed more alliteratively by stating that "manners are but minor morals."[3]

Academics may be prone to overlook the connection because too many view scholarly inquiry as a competition in which you score points by refuting others rather than a cooperative enterprise in which participants reason together to enhance understanding. Indeed, whenever colleagues move the process forward, they deserve gratitude.

Even when criticisms are offered at a professional lecture, they should begin on a positive note, if only to thank the speaker for raising provocative issues. Such politeness will not diminish the significance of any challenge but will reinforce the principle that criticism is consistent with courtesy.

Academic life has its share of travails. Those would be lessened, however, if professors emphasized not only the importance of correctness but also a concern for kindness.

2. Thomas Hobbes, *Leviathan* (Cleveland and New York: The World Publishing Company, 1963), 122.

3. John Dewey, *Democracy and Education: The Middle Works of John Dewey, 1899–1924,* ed. Jo Ann Boydston (Carbondale, IL: Southern Illinois University Press, 1980), 9:22.

# 24

## MY PATHWAY

IN WRITING THIS BOOK, I have found myself reflecting on my nearly fifty years as a faculty member. I hope that sharing a few highlights of that experience may provide useful background for understanding my outlook.

### I

One fall morning in 1965, when I was completing my doctoral work in Columbia University's Graduate Department of Philosophy, the secretary asked if I would be willing to be interviewed for a position the next year at Vassar College. I hesitated because I had not anticipated a post at a women's college (only later did Vassar become co-ed), but fortunately the secretary persisted and scheduled an interview conducted by the long-time chair of the Vassar department, Vernon Venable. In those days, openings were not publicly announced, and Professor Venable's search procedure consisted of visiting potential candidates only at Harvard, Yale, and Columbia.

During our brief meeting, he asked whether I was a Wittgensteinian. Although not entirely sure of his meaning, I replied that I wasn't. That answer turned out to be helpful, because, as Professor Venable subsequently explained, he didn't care for the work of Wittgenstein. Afterwards, he asked me to examine the Vassar catalogue and indicate which philosophy courses I would prefer to teach, which I would be willing to teach, and which I would not want to teach.

That task was not difficult until I came to a course titled "Philosophy of Education." I had not heard of this subject and wondered into which category I should place it. I reasoned fallaciously that because I was interested both in philosophy and in education (having taught religious studies to grade school students), I would also be interested in philosophy of education. Therefore, I listed it among the subjects I would prefer to teach.

Little did I realize that expressing enthusiasm for that course would be a primary reason I would be chosen for the position. In fact, the department was required to offer the course every semester to meet the needs of the education students, and as I later learned, no member of the philosophy faculty or any other applicant wanted to teach it. Ironically, the field became a specialty of mine, and soon after leaving Vassar, having taught the course four times, I edited my own anthology, which still remains in use.[1]

Before I began at Vassar, though, I had a free semester, and my dissertation advisor, Richard Taylor,[2] recommended me to the faculty at Dartmouth College, where someone was needed for one semester to teach discussion sections of the introductory course. I gratefully accepted an offer and spent a delightful term in Hanover, New Hampshire, where I heard captivating lectures to the students by Professors Willis Doney, Timothy Duggan, and Bernard Gert. All three welcomed me, and as a beginner I was grateful for their cordiality.

The department sponsored colloquia, and I still remember the visit by the eminent historian of philosophy, Father Frederick Copleston. After his talk, he spent the rest of the evening answering with remarkable ease complex questions posed by faculty

---

1. Steven M. Cahn, ed., *Classic and Contemporary Readings in the Philosophy of Education,* Second Edition (New York: Oxford University Press, 2012).

2. Richard Taylor's immense influence on my career is discussed in Steven M. Cahn, *From Student to Scholar: A Candid Guide to Becoming a Professor,* Second Edition (Eugene, OR: Wipf and Stock Publishers, 2024), 100–104.

members seeking his assistance in handling especially challenging interpretative problems in the history of philosophy. Copleston's mastery was astounding.


## II


When autumn came, I arrived at Vassar, and the two years I spent there proved to be among the happiest of my academic career. The students were first-rate and enthusiastic, while the faculty was knowledgeable and amiable. Indeed, I developed a special relationship with three members of the department.

One was John O'Connor, who later became executive director of the American Philosophical Association. John had earned his PhD at Harvard, while serving as a teaching assistant for both W. V. O. Quine and John Rawls. My colleague was an amazingly sharp thinker yet easy to talk to. I learned much from our many conversations and enjoyed evenings in his company.

Another who became a long-standing friend was Garrett Vander Veer, who earned his degree at Yale, where he had been a student of the eminent idealist philosopher Brand Blanshard. While Garry and I had different philosophical backgrounds, I admired his academic integrity, the unwillingness to compromise reasonable standards. His comments at department meetings were invariably insightful.

A third philosopher of note was Frank Tillman, to whom I had been introduced when we both attended the philosophical discussion group that met at Richard Taylor's apartment during his years at Columbia. After I had been at Vassar for a few weeks, Frank invited me to his large office and showed me piles of materials that he hoped to shape into a reader in aesthetics to be published by Harper & Row, for whom he worked as a consultant. He asked if I might help him complete the volume and become its co-editor. I had no experience with such work but was pleased to participate. Eventually the book became my first anthology, introducing me to the world of college publishing and resulting in my lifelong interest in such projects.[3]

## III

Although I enjoyed the ambiance at Vassar, I had always hoped to return to New York City; hence, I was delighted when I received an invitation from Sidney Hook to join the faculty at New York University's Washington Square College in Greenwich Village.

The next five years, 1968–1973, were a time of disruption to our country and NYU, but for me they were a period of growth and excitement. I taught large undergraduate courses, sometimes with as many as a hundred or more students, took on graduate seminars with talented future scholars, some of whom would become nationally known, and accepted departmental and college-wide administrative assignments. Chief among these was serving as head of the school's Educational Policy Committee, which was responsible for approving every department's proposed curricular changes. My responsibilities led me to meet many of the College's leading faculty members, an opportunity I relished.

Within the Department, I welcomed working with its longtime head, Professor Hook, whose writings I greatly admired. While he was a fierce debater concerning the issues of the day, he was always generous to students and colleagues. Although the mailboxes of the other members of the department were virtually empty, his was invariably stuffed with correspondence from around the world. Yet his celebrity mattered no more to him than teaching a class or providing a letter of recommendation. I remain grateful for his many kindnesses.

3. Frank A. Tillman and Steven M. Cahn, eds., *Philosophy of Art and Aesthetics: From Plato to Wittgenstein* (New York: Harper & Row, 1969). Although the book eventually went out of print, it provided the structure for Steven M. Cahn and Aaron Meskin, eds., *Aesthetics: A Comprehensive Anthology,* (Malden, MA: Blackwell Publishing, 2008) with a widely used second edition in 2020 edited by Steven M. Cahn, Stephanie Ross and Sandra Shapshay.

Almost every day I ate lunch with my colleague James Rachels. In New York City most faculty members do not spend much time at school but treat the entire City as a campus. Jim and I, however, were regularly in our offices, and, as we were about the same age and at the same stage of our careers, we conversed endlessly about philosophy, academic life, and our colleagues. He was remarkably affable, easy-going, and straightforward. The trait most foreign to him was pomposity. Typical was his reply to someone who asked about "films he had attended": "I don't attend films, " he replied. "I go to movies."

Unfortunately, after we had been at NYU for several years, the school suffered a financial crisis and the administrators, seeking to reduce the size of the faculty, urged that any professor able to leave should do so. Jim decided to accept an offer from the University of Miami, and when he departed, I was willing to consider other possibilities.

## III

An unusual one appeared at the University of Vermont, which advertised for a department chair. When the head of their search committee, noted psychologist George Albee, unexpectedly came to New York to visit me, I learned of a strange situation. Until several years before, few philosophers were on the faculty, and they were part of a single philosophy and religion department. When the University rapidly increased in size, the department did as well. Unfortunately, the process was handled without regard for appropriate academic procedures. The result was a large but undistinguished group that considered itself estranged from the contemporary philosophical scene. They were soon at loggerheads with the administration, and Professor Albee was asked to head an ad hoc committee to find someone who could lead the development of a first-class independent philosophy department. He wondered if I might be willing to accept the assignment.

Had the situation at NYU been settled, I am sure I would have turned him down. But the challenge of building a strong department was appealing, and with some naïveté I decided to pursue the opportunity. When eventually a formal offer was made, I accepted.

The task, however, proved far more difficult than I had imagined. The Dean had invited me without the support of most of the faculty; they had opposed every outside candidate, and, with a couple of exceptions, the members resisted evaluation by usual academic standards. The only positive feature of the situation was that quite a few of the department's faculty were untenured and subject to annual reappointment. After speaking with each of them at length and assessing their records, I recommended that four not be invited to return the following year.

The matter became a cause célèbre. Yet after several months of turmoil, the administration backed my recommendation. Three of the four were not reappointed, and the fourth was warned that unless he soon obtained his long-sought doctoral degree, he would not be continued; the following year he voluntarily departed.

Thus, the department needed at least three new faculty, and I had the primary responsibility for choosing them. The advertisement I placed yielded more than 700 applications. I studied each, then at the Eastern Division meeting of the American Philosophical Association, I conducted interviews by myself and invited the most promising candidates to campus.

Eventually, after convincing the Dean to allow four appointments, I chose Patricia Kitcher, Philip Kitcher, William Mann, and George Sher. I doubt if ever in my life I made a wiser academic decision. While their philosophical interests varied widely, all were superb teachers and future leading researchers who would eventually hold chairs in philosophy. At the time I met them, though, their total publication record consisted of one essay. (Since then, they have written more than 25 books and 300 articles.)

Each of my new colleagues was enormously conscientious and committed to work tirelessly to build the department, locally and nationally. The task was arduous, but our efforts succeeded, and the University of Vermont gained a reputation for excellence in philosophy that remains to this day. Indeed, any list of the strongest undergraduate philosophy departments in the United States invariably includes the University of Vermont.

We conducted searches with the utmost care, and our appointments were so strong that over time at least eight of those who joined the department went on to professorships in leading doctoral programs. Given that for a half century, thousands of undergraduates at the University of Vermont have had the opportunity to study philosophy with the guidance of an outstanding faculty, I consider the building of that department, however onerous, to have been a major accomplishment.

## IV

Subsequently, I was offered the opportunity to enter the world of foundations, where during a five-year period I worked at the Exxon Education Foundation, the Rockefeller Foundation, and the National Endowment for the Humanities.[4] Eventually, I returned to academic life as an administrator at the City University of New York Graduate Center, where I served for nearly a decade as Dean of Graduate Studies, then Provost and Vice President for Academic Affairs, then Acting President.[5] During that time I also held a professorship in the Philosophy Program, where I continued to teach part-time and engage in research. Ultimately, I left the administration and for the next two decades served as a full-time professor of philosophy and urban studies, teaching graduate courses, conversing frequently with my friend David Rosenthal, the outstanding philosopher of mind, and serving as the advisor for many doctoral students writing their dissertations.

The students with whom I worked did more than they knew to enhance the sense of satisfaction I have found with my academic career. While most have disappeared from my view, quite a number have stayed in touch, and nine have worked with me as colleagues on book projects: Maureen Eckert, Robert Gurland,

4. For an account of that experience, see Steven M. Cahn, *The Road Travelled and Other Essays* (Eugene, OR: Wipf and Stock Publishers, 2019, 91–95.

5. Details can be found in Cahn, 95–98.

Tziporah Kasachkoff, Peter Markie, David Shatz, Robert Talisse, the late Andrea Tschemplik, Carissa Véliz and Christine Vitrano. Having now retired to write and edit, I treasure the time I spent as a teacher.

# WORKS BY STEVEN M. CAHN

### Books Authored

*Fate, Logic, and Time*
    Yale University Press, 1967
    Ridgeview Publishing Company, 1982
    Wipf and Stock Publishers, 2004
*A New Introduction to Philosophy*
    Harper & Row, 1971
    University Press of America, 1986
    Wipf and Stock Publishers, 2004
*The Eclipse of Excellence: A Critique of American Higher Education*
    (Foreword by Charles Frankel)
    Public Affairs Press, 1973
    Wipf and Stock Publishers, 2004
*Education and the Democratic Ideal*
    Nelson-Hall Company, 1979
    Wipf and Stock Publishers, 2004
*Saints and Scamps: Ethics in Academia*
    Rowman & Littlefield, 1986
    Revised Edition, 1994
    25th Anniversary Edition, 2011
    (Foreword by Thomas H. Powell)
*Philosophical Explorations: Freedom, God, and Goodness*
    Prometheus Books, 1989
*Puzzles & Perplexities: Collected Essays*
    Rowman & Littlefield, 2002
    Second Edition, 2007

*God, Reason, and Religion*
Thomson/Wadsworth, 2006
*From Student to Scholar: A Candid Guide to Becoming a Professor*
(Foreword by Catharine R. Stimpson)
Columbia University Press, 2008
Second Edition, Wipf and Stock Publishers, 2024
*Polishing Your Prose: How to Turn First Drafts Into Finished Work*
(with Victor L. Cahn)
(Foreword by Mary Ann Caws)
Columbia University Press, 2013
*Happiness and Goodness: Philosophical Reflections on Living Well*
(with Christine Vitrano)
(Foreword by Robert B. Talisse)
Columbia University Press, 2015
*Religion Within Reason*
Columbia University Press, 2017
Second Edition, Wipf and Stock Publishers, 2025
*Teaching Philosophy: A Guide*
Routledge, 2018
*Inside Academia: Professors, Politics, and Policies*
Rutgers University Press, 2019
*The Road Traveled and Other Essays*
Wipf and Stock Publishers, 2019
*Philosophical Adventures*
Broadview Press, 2019
*A Philosopher's Journey: Essays from Six Decades*
Wipf and Stock Publishers, 2020
*Philosophical Debates*
Wipf and Stock Publishers, 2021
*Navigating Academic Life: How the System Works*
Routledge, 2021
*Professors as Teachers*
Wipf and Stock Publishers, 2022
*Exploring Academic Ethics*
Wipf and Stock Publishers, 2024
*Pathways Through Academia*
Wipf and Stock Publishers, 2025

## Books Edited

*Philosophy of Art and Aesthetics: From Plato to Wittgenstein*
    (with Frank A. Tillman)
    Harper & Row, 1969
*The Philosophical Foundations of Education*
    Harper & Row, 1970
*Philosophy of Religion*
    Harper & Row, 1970
*Classics of Western Philosophy*
    Hackett Publishing Company, 1977
    Second Edition, 1985
    Third Edition, 1990
    Fourth Edition, 1995
    Fifth Edition, 1999
    Sixth Edition, 2003
    Seventh Edition, 2007
    Eighth Edition, 2012
*New Studies in the Philosophy of John Dewey*
    University Press of New England, 1977
*Scholars Who Teach: The Art of College Teaching*
    Nelson-Hall Company, 1978
    Wipf and Stock Publishers, 2004
*Contemporary Philosophy of Religion*
    (with David Shatz)
    Oxford University Press, 1982
*Reason at Work: Introductory Readings in Philosophy*
    (with Patricia Kitcher and George Sher)
    Harcourt Brace Jovanovich, 1984
    Second Edition, 1990
    Third Edition (also with Peter J. Markie), 1995
*Morality, Responsibility, and the University: Studies in Academic Ethics*
    Temple University Press, 1990
*Affirmative Action and the University: A Philosophical Inquiry*
    Temple University Press, 1993
*Twentieth-Century Ethical Theory*
    (with Joram G. Haber)
    Prentice Hall, 1995

*The Affirmative Action Debate*
    Routledge, 1995
    Second Edition, 2002
*Classics of Modern Political Theory: Machiavelli to Mill*
    Oxford University Press, 1997
*Classic and Contemporary Readings in the Philosophy of Education*
    McGraw Hill, 1997
    Second Edition, Oxford University Press, 2012
*Ethics: History, Theory, and Contemporary Issues*
    (with Peter Markie)
    Oxford University Press, 1998
    Second Edition, 2002
    Third Edition, 2006
    Fourth Edition, 2009
    Fifth Edition, 2012
    Sixth Edition, 2015
    Seventh Edition, 2020
*Exploring Philosophy: An Introductory Anthology*
    Oxford University Press, 2000
    Second Edition, 2005
    Third Edition, 2009
    Fourth Edition, 2012
    Fifth Edition, 2015
    Sixth Edition, 2018
    Seventh Edition, 2021
    Eighth Edition, 2024
*Classics of Political and Moral Philosophy*
    Oxford University Press, 2002
    Second Edition, 2012
*Questions About God: Today's Philosophers Ponder the Divine*
    (with David Shatz)
    Oxford University Press, 2002
*Morality and Public Policy*
    (with Tziporah Kasachkoff)
    Prentice Hall, 2003

*Knowledge and Reality*
  (with Maureen Eckert and Robert Buckley)
  Prentice Hall, 2003
*Philosophy for the 21st Century: A Comprehensive Reader*
  Oxford University Press, 2003
*Ten Essential Texts in the Philosophy of Religion*
  Oxford University Press, 2005
*Political Philosophy: The Essential Texts*
  Oxford University Press, 2005
  Second Edition, 2011
  Third Edition, 2015
  Fourth Edition, 2022
*Philosophical Horizons: Introductory Readings*
  (with Maureen Eckert)
  Thomson/Wadsworth, 2006
  Second Edition, 2012
*Aesthetics: A Comprehensive Anthology*
  (with Aaron Meskin)
  Blackwell, 2008
  Second Edition (with Stephanie Ross and Sandra Shapshay), 2020
*Happiness: Classic and Contemporary Readings*
  (with Christine Vitrano)
  Oxford University Press, 2008
*The Meaning of Life, 3rd Edition: A Reader*
  (with E. M. Klemke)
  Oxford University Press, 2008
  Fourth Edition, 2018
*Seven Masterpieces of Philosophy*
  Pearson Longman, 2008
*The Elements of Philosophy: Readings from Past and Present*
  (with Tamar Szabó Gendler and Susanna Siegel)
  Oxford University Press, 2008
*Exploring Philosophy of Religion: An Introductory Anthology*
  Oxford University Press, 2009
  Second Edition, 2016

*Exploring Ethics: An Introductory Anthology*
    Oxford University Press, 2009
    Second Edition, 2011
    Third Edition, 2014
    Fourth Edition, 2017
    Fifth Edition, 2020
    Sixth Edition, 2023

*Philosophy of Education: The Essential Texts*
    Routledge, 2009

*Political Problems*
    (with Robert B. Talisse)
    Prentice Hall, 2011

*Thinking About Logic: Classic Essays*
    (with Robert B. Talisse and Scott F. Aikin)
    Westview Press, 2011

*Fate, Time, and Language: An Essay on Free Will by David Foster Wallace*
    (with Maureen Eckert)
    Columbia University Press, 2011

*Moral Problems in Higher Education*
    Temple University Press, 2011
    Wipf and Stock Publishers, 2021

*Political Philosophy in the Twenty-First Century*
    (with Robert B. Talisse)
    Westview Press, 2013

*Portraits of American Philosophy*
    Rowman & Littlefield, 2013

*Reason and Religions: Philosophy Looks at the World's Religious Beliefs*
    Wadsworth/Cengage Learning, 2014

*Freedom and the Self: Essays on the Philosophy of David Foster Wallace*
    (with Maureen Eckert)
    Columbia University Press, 2015

*The World of Philosophy*
    Oxford University Press, 2016
    Second Edition, 2019

*Principles of Moral Philosophy: Classic and Contemporary Approaches*
    (with Andrew T. Forcehimes)
    Oxford University Press, 2017

*Foundations of Moral Philosophy: Readings in Metaethics*
 (with Andrew T. Forcehimes)
 Oxford University Press, 2017
*Exploring Moral Problems: An Introductory Anthology*
 (with Andrew T. Forcehimes)
 Oxford University Press, 2018
*Philosophers in the Classroom: Essays on Teaching*
 (with Alexandra Bradner and Andrew Mills)
 Hackett Publishing Company, 2018
*An Annotated Kant: Groundwork for the Metaphysics of Morals*
 Rowman & Littlefield, 2020
*The Democracy Reader: From Classical to Contemporary Philosophy*
 (with Andrew T. Forcehimes and Robert B. Talisse)
 Rowman & Littlefield, 2021
*Academic Ethics Today: Problems, Policies, and Perspectives
 on University Life*
 Rowman & Littlefield, 2022
*Privacy*
 (with Carissa Véliz)
 Wiley-Blackwell, 2023
*Understanding Kant's Groundwork*
 Hackett Publishing Company, 2023
*Bronx Socrates: Portrait of a Legendary Teacher*
 Wipf and Stock Publishers, 2024

# ABOUT THE AUTHOR

Steven M. Cahn is Professor Emeritus of Philosophy at the City University of New York Graduate Center, where he served for nearly a decade as Provost and Vice President for Academic Affairs, then as Acting President.

He was born in Springfield, Massachusetts, in 1942. His early years were devoted to music, and he studied piano with Herbert Stessin of the Juilliard School and the noted chamber music artist Artur Balsam. He also became a professional organist under the tutelage of the eminent composer Isadore Freed. At Dr. Cahn's high school, Woodmere Academy (now Lawrence Woodmere Academy), he was principal clarinetist in the school's celebrated concert band.

After earning an AB from Columbia College in 1963 and PhD in philosophy from Columbia University in 1966, Dr. Cahn taught at Dartmouth College, Vassar College, New York University, the University of Rochester, and the University of Vermont, where he chaired the Department of Philosophy and led the successful effort to build what remains one of the country's most highly rated undergraduate programs.

He served as a program officer at the Exxon Education Foundation, as Acting Director for Humanities at the Rockefeller Foundation, and as the first Director of General Programs at the National Endowment for the Humanities. He formerly chaired the American Philosophical Association's Committee on the Teaching of Philosophy, was the Association's delegate to the American Council of Learned Societies, and was longtime President of the

John Dewey Foundation, where he proposed and brought to fruition the John Dewey Lectures, now delivered at every national meeting of the American Philosophical Association.

He has presented numerous addresses at colleges and universities throughout the United States, including the first Naumberg Memorial Lecture at UCLA, the Minerva Lecture at Union College, the convocation address at Florida International University, and a keynote speech to the Kenan Convocation at the University of North Carolina at Chapel Hill. He has also spoken at meetings of numerous organizations, including the College Entrance Examination Board, the American Board of Internal Medicine, the American Association of State Colleges and Universities, the National Association of Academic Affairs Administrators, and both the Northeastern and Midwestern Association of Graduate Schools.

He is the author of more than twenty books and editor of over fifty others. He has also served as general editor of four multivolume series: *Blackwell Philosophy Guides, Blackwell Readings in Philosophy, Issues in Academic Ethics,* and *Critical Essays on the Classics.*

His numerous articles have appeared in a broad spectrum of publications, including *The Journal of Philosophy, The Chronicle of Higher Education, Shakespeare Newsletter, The American Journal of Medicine, The New Republic,* and *The New York Times.*

A collection of essays written in his honor, edited by two of his former doctoral students, Robert B. Talisse of Vanderbilt University and Maureen Eckert of the University of Massachusetts Dartmouth, is titled *A Teacher's Life: Essays for Steven M. Cahn* (Rowman & Littlefield). His professional autobiography appears in his book *The Road Traveled and Other Essays.*

# Index

www.ingramcontent.com/pod-product-compliance
Lightning Source LLC
Chambersburg PA
CBHW052134090426
42741CB00009B/2077